Helen MacGregor & Stephen

Singing Times Tables

BOOK 1

Songs, chants, raps and games for teaching times tables

CONTENTS

SINGING TIMES TABLES BOOK 1 • HELEN MACGREGOR & STEPHEN CHADWICK © 2013 A&C BLACK PUBLISHERS LTD • www.bloomsbury.com/music

INTRODUCTION

Singing Times Tables Book 1 is a resource full of motivational and creative ideas for learning and understanding the mathematical processes of times tables through fun songs, chants, raps and games. The book covers the 2, 3, 4, 5 and 10 times tables and is suitable for teaching 5–7 year olds.

As adults, we all know how useful it is to be able to instantly recall and use times tables in everyday situations, from calculating costs when shopping to adjusting measurements for DIY or cookery. If we can learn our tables thoroughly by rote at an early age and understand how to apply this knowledge, we have immediate access to them for life!

This resource gives stimulating ideas for aural, visual and kinaesthetic learning through songs, chants and activities that promote:

★ rote learning of the 2, 3, 4, 5 and 10 times tables or any table of your choice;
★ understanding through exploration and fun, practical maths games;
★ use of a variety of mathematical language;
★ recall of tables facts in games and tests.

Cross-curricular links

Many of the songs and chants have cross-curricular links that enable the songs and activities to be integrated into topic work. In Section 2, each times table is accompanied by an imaginative theme or story. The extension activities include ways to link with other subjects, for example: Art (*Fingerfish*) and Design and Technology (*Robot X*). Some of the songs include opportunities for using skills in Drama (*Two by two*) and Music (*Jangle triangle*). All of the rhyming chants and songs can be used to develop or reinforce literacy skills.

The CD/CD-ROM

There are two parts to the CD/CD-ROM – the audio tracks and the graphic resources. The audio tracks section (for use in a conventional CD player) contains a performance track and a backing track for each of the songs, chants or raps (see full track listing on p64). The performance track can be used to help you and the children to learn the song. The backing track allows you to adapt the song or chant, and helps to improve memory skills. Many of the songs and chants can, once learnt, also be performed unaccompanied, particularly those that form part of a game.

The CD icons at the top of each activity give the audio track numbers:

 performance track number

 backing track number

The graphic resources section (for use in a computer) contains the song lyrics and all the relevant times table charts. It also contains displays, templates and worksheets. All these resources can be printed out or displayed on a whiteboard.

Displays, templates and worksheets

Each song has a photocopiable songsheet that can be used with the children to enhance their literacy skills. A set of photocopiable displays, templates and worksheets that support the activities is included on pages 46–63. All these graphic resources are supplied on the CD/CD-ROM for access on a computer.

The template icons at the top of each activity show the page number where the corresponding template can be found:

 template page number

Teaching focus

The teaching focus of each song, chant or rap can be found at the bottom of each page.

About the activities

The teaching notes give step-by-step suggestions of ways to introduce and teach the songs, chants or raps to the children. It is recommended that the children learn the songs and chants aurally, though you will also want to show them the tables displayed on the songsheets in Section 1 when learning the song.

Extending the activity

Use these ideas to make the activities more challenging, eg by exploring the times table to promote understanding, by using and applying the tables knowledge, by using a different times table, or by testing recall.

Section 1
Learning the tables

This section has a song for each of the tables appropriate for the age group 5–7. Each song is written in a different musical style and the theme relates to the number patterns of the table, eg the four times table is taught through the idea of a procession of four-legged beasts. These themes can also be linked with cross-curricular work, eg science.

Section 2
Practising any times table

Each of these chants offers a fun way to recite any times table of your choice. In *Copycat mice*, the children take on the voices of the animals to learn through copying. In *The giant's table*, the children practise times tables calculations needed to run the giant's castle. The performance track demonstrates how the words and rhythms of any times table can be performed with the music, eg the three times table is used as an example in *Tables on parade* as the sergeant major drills the troops.

Section 3
Investigating number patterns

These songs, chants and raps each relate to a single times table and provide creative opportunities to explore and understand the mathematical processes of multiplication and division, eg *Two by two* encourages play with small world animals to understand how counting in twos relates to the two times table. In *Pond life*, the children listen to patterns of animal sounds and explore the relationship between different times tables using a number grid.

Section 4
Tests

These songs and chants give plenty of opportunities for testing any times table in fun and engaging ways, eg while moving to a hoedown or by memorising using the aural prompts in *Sound effects tables*.

Milk bottle deliveries

It's very early in the morning and the milkman is on his rounds delivering bottles of milk to the houses.

The first house doesn't want any milk. All the others want two bottles each. The milkman picks up one bottle in each hand and puts them both on the doorstep. As he works, he sings his two times table to help him count.

★ Listen to performance track 1 to hear the milkman sing the two times table as he works. Show the class an enlarged copy of the songsheet (opposite and CD), then sing along with the milkman:

> Zero times two is zero,
> One times two is two…

★ Practise saying the two times table, then sing the whole song with backing track 2.

EXTENDING THE ACTIVITY

★ Use the milk bottle templates (p46 and CD) to make 24 bottles of milk from card. Choose a child to act out the role of the milkman and deliver the milk bottles two by two as you all sing the song.

★ Give the children copies of the 24-bottle milk crate (p46 and CD) and explain that the twelve houses might have different types of milk, each with a different colour bottle top, eg
~ four houses have green-top milk bottles
~ six houses have red-top milk bottles
~ two houses have blue-top milk bottles

How can they organise the bottles in the crate so they always pick up two of the same colour? Ask them to find different ways to colour in the pairs of green-top, red-top and blue-top milk bottles to show their answers.

★ Test the children's knowledge of the table by giving them the worksheet showing streets with different numbers of houses (p47 and CD). How many bottles are delivered to each street?

★ To explore other times tables, change the number of bottles per house, eg three. Use the worksheets again to calculate the total numbers of bottles per street.

WHAT YOU WILL NEED

★ An enlarged copy of the songsheet (opposite and CD)

Extension activity:

★ Milk bottle template (p46 and CD)
★ A milk crate template (p46 and CD)
★ Houses worksheet (p47 and CD)

Teaching focus
• Learning and exploring the two times table.

SINGING TIMES TABLES BOOK 1 • HELEN MACGREGOR & STEPHEN CHADWICK © 2013 A&C BLACK PUBLISHERS LTD • www.bloomsbury.com/music

Milk bottle deliveries

0 x 2 = 0

1 x 2 = 2

2 x 2 = 4

3 x 2 = 6

4 x 2 = 8

5 x 2 = 10

6 x 2 = 12

7 x 2 = 14

8 x 2 = 16

9 x 2 = 18

10 x 2 = 20

11 x 2 = 22

12 x 2 = 24

Three is a magic number

It's time for the witches' and wizards' Annual Conference and Ball. They need to learn twelve new spells — one for every month of the new year. To make each spell work properly, they must wave their wands a specific number of times. For January's spell, they only need to wave their wands three times, but by December they will need to wave them three times for each of the twelve months, ie 3 x 12 = 36 times! Can they learn their tables well enough to get each spell right?

★ Display an enlarged copy of the songsheet (opposite and CD).

★ Learn the melody by listening to performance track 3. Join in with the three times table:

> *Zero times three is zero,*
> *One times three is three…*

★ When the children are confident, sing the whole song with backing track 4.

EXTENDING THE ACTIVITY

★ Divide the class into twelve groups and ask each to write a short spell so that there is a spell for each month of the year, eg

> *Hocus pocus, flee fly flo,*
> *Make this little lollipop grow!*

★ Attach the spells to a large wall calendar (p48 and CD), allocating one to each month of the year.

★ Have fun reciting each spell and working out the correct number of times to wave the magic wands to make the spell work!

★ Use the calendar to test the children's knowledge. Recite one of the spells and challenge the children to call out the correct number of wand waves they need to make at the end of the spell.

WHAT YOU WILL NEED

★ An enlarged copy of the songsheet (opposite and CD)

★ An enlarged copy of the wall calendar display (p48 and CD)

Extension activity:

★ Paper and pens for writing spells

Teaching focus
• Learning and exploring the three times table.

Three is a magic number

0 x 3 =   0

1 x 3 =   3

2 x 3 =   6

3 x 3 =   9

4 x 3 = 12

5 x 3 = 15

6 x 3 = 18

7 x 3 = 21

8 x 3 = 24

9 x 3 = 27

10 x 3 = 30

11 x 3 = 33

12 x 3 = 36

Procession of four-legged beasts

PERFORMANCE 5 BACKING 6 49

A four-legged beast is going for a long walk to look for water. As the beast walks along, other four-legged beasts join in, one by one, until there is a procession of twelve.

★ Show the children an enlarged copy of the songsheet (opposite and CD). Play performance track 5 to learn the melody:

 Zero times four is zero,
 One times four is four…

★ When the children are familiar with the song, use backing track 6 to perform the four times table from memory.

EXTENDING THE ACTIVITY

★ Create a large classroom wall frieze with the twelve chosen animals in the procession (p49 and CD), or ask the children to choose and draw their own animals.

★ Place a multiple on each animal (4 8 12…48) to show the total number of legs as the procession extends.

★ Make animal masks, then act out the procession in a large space, with children taking the role of the animals, moving slowly on hands and knees to illustrate the number pattern. Add more children to extend the pattern and calculate the multiples: 52 56 60…

★ Play this *Four-legged beasts* game to test the children's knowledge of the four times table. Divide up the whole class into random groups of different sizes. Can each group work out the total number of animal legs (ie the number of children in the group multiplied by four) without counting to check? Keep changing the groups around to practise quick recall of the table.

WHAT YOU WILL NEED

★ An enlarged copy of the songsheet (opposite and CD)

Extension activities:

★ Pictures of twelve four-legged animals to make a wall frieze of the procession (use the templates on p49 and CD or let the children draw their own)

★ Materials for children to make their own animal masks

★ Space to act out the procession

Teaching focus
• Learning and exploring the four times table.

Procession of four-legged beasts

0 x 4 = 0

1 x 4 = 4

2 x 4 = 8

3 x 4 = 12

4 x 4 = 16

5 x 4 = 20

6 x 4 = 24

7 x 4 = 28

8 x 4 = 32

9 x 4 = 36

10 x 4 = 40

11 x 4 = 44

12 x 4 = 48

Five finger-snakes

Twelve snake charmers are sitting in the sun playing their pipes. Each has a basket of five snakes that rise up and dance to the music, one basket at a time. Count the snakes by practising the five times table as they dance.

★ Display an enlarged copy of the songsheet (opposite and CD) and play performance track 7 to learn the song:

> *Zero times five is zero,*
> *One times five is five…*

★ Choose twelve children (the snake charmers) and number them from 1 to 12. As the class sings, the snake charmers start wiggling the fingers of one hand (the snakes) to show that their basket of snakes has joined in with the dance.

★ Sing the whole song with backing track 8, giving other children the opportunity to illustrate the snakes with wiggling fingers.

EXTENDING THE ACTIVITY

★ Choose six children to stand in a line facing the class. As everyone sings, help the six children join in one by one, wiggling the fingers of one hand, then the other to match the number pattern of the times table, until the group is showing 60 wiggling snakes (all six pairs of hands). Compare the number facts with the twelve-children version. Why are there only six children this time?

★ Design twelve colourful baskets (p50 and CD), each with five wiggly dancing snakes, and display these to illustrate and practise the five times table.

★ Try performing the snake dance with the ten times table. How many snakes would you have at the end of the dance if there were ten snakes per basket?

WHAT YOU WILL NEED

★ An enlarged copy of the songsheet (opposite and CD)

Extension activity:

★ Twelve colourful baskets and five wiggly dancing snakes (p50 and CD)

Teaching focus
• Learning and exploring the five times table.

SINGING TIMES TABLES BOOK 1 • HELEN MACGREGOR & STEPHEN CHADWICK © 2013 A&C BLACK PUBLISHERS LTD • www.bloomsbury.com/mus

Five finger-snakes

$$0 \times 5 = 0$$
$$1 \times 5 = 5$$
$$2 \times 5 = 10$$
$$3 \times 5 = 15$$
$$4 \times 5 = 20$$
$$5 \times 5 = 25$$
$$6 \times 5 = 30$$
$$7 \times 5 = 35$$
$$8 \times 5 = 40$$
$$9 \times 5 = 45$$
$$10 \times 5 = 50$$
$$11 \times 5 = 55$$
$$12 \times 5 = 60$$

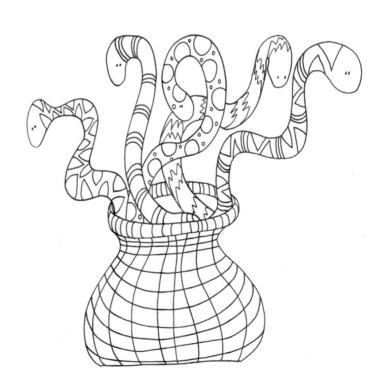

Finger-fish

A diver is exploring the ocean, looking for the colourful, imaginary 'finger-fish'. Every ten metres the diver descends, she meets a new shoal of ten finger-fish.

★ Choose twelve children to stand in a line. Ask the first child to hold up all ten fingers. Repeat, adding one child at a time, as everyone practises counting in tens: 10 20 30…120.

★ Explain the story of the diver and ask the children to 'swim' their finger-fish along to the music, joining in one by one to match the pattern in the times table as you listen to performance track 9.

★ Learn the ten times table song using the performance track, then perform it with backing track 10.

EXTENDING THE ACTIVITY

★ Make a vertical wall frieze to illustrate the ten times table using the diver story as a stimulus.

Using the templates (p51 and CD), make a diver from card and twelve shoals of ten finger-fish. Alternatively, ask the children to make their own finger-fish shoals with fingerprints, adding fins, tails and eyes for each fish.

On a large vertical chart, make a depth mark every ten metres starting at 0 for surface level and ending at 120. Add one shoal of fish at each ten-metre mark.

★ Use the chart to illustrate the ten times table, counting the total depth travelled and fish seen at each ten-metre marker. Invite a child to lead the song by moving the diver down the chart as everyone sings.

★ Play this *Diver* game to test the children's knowledge and recall. Choose a child to be the diver and ask them to make the figure descend to their chosen depth. Can the others say how many finger-fish the diver has seen?

★ Using the five-armed starfish templates (p51 and CD), make twelve starfish and place one at each ten-metre mark. Calculate how many starfish arms the diver has seen at different depths, eg at 30 metres there have been 3 sets of 5 arms = 15 arms.

WHAT YOU WILL NEED

Extension activity:

★ Materials to make a diving wall frieze

★ Twelve finger-fish shoals, twelve starfish and a diver (p51 and CD)

★ Paints and other decorating materials if the children are making the finger-fish shoals and starfish themselves

Teaching focus
• Learning and exploring the ten times table.

Finger-fish

0 x 10 =   0

1 x 10 = 10

2 x 10 = 20

3 x 10 = 30

4 x 10 = 40

5 x 10 = 50

6 x 10 = 60

7 x 10 = 70

8 x 10 = 80

9 x 10 = 90

10 x 10 = 100

11 x 10 = 110

12 x 10 = 120

The giant's table

The giant from *Jack and the beanstalk* needs to practise counting how much money he has made from the golden eggs laid by his magic hen. He is slowly sorting and counting his golden coins.

★ Choose a times table to practise, eg the two times table. Display an enlarged copy of the chosen times table if needed. Using deep giant voices, practise chanting the table followed by its multiples along with performance track 11:

> *Zero times two is zero,*
> *One times two is two…*

EXTENDING THE ACTIVITY

★ Use backing track 12 to practise other vocabulary for saying the tables, eg

> *Nought times two is zero,*
> *One two is two...*

★ Give the children play coins (p52 and CD) to handle and count in twos as they say the chant with the performance track or without the track during paired or small group work. If there are more than 24 coins, can they continue the sequence, sorting the extra coins into twos to find the total?

★ Investigate other times tables calculations needed to run the giant's castle, eg

~ Two times table: how many enormous socks does the giant need in a week if he wears a clean pair every day?
~ Three times table: if he has three eggs a day (except on Sunday when he has a huge bowl of porridge), how many eggs does he need to cook for a whole week's breakfasts?
~ Five times table: how many golden coins does he need to fill five sacks if each sack holds twelve coins?
~ Ten times table: how many cobwebs are there in the castle if there are ten in each of the twelve rooms?

WHAT YOU WILL NEED

★ An enlarged copy of the chosen times table songsheet if needed (opposite or relevant songsheet on CD)

Extension activity:

★ Sets of play coins (p52 and CD)

Teaching focus
• Any times table.

The giant's table
Example: two times table

$0 \times 2 = 0$

$1 \times 2 = 2$

$2 \times 2 = 4$

$3 \times 2 = 6$

$4 \times 2 = 8$

$5 \times 2 = 10$

$6 \times 2 = 12$

$7 \times 2 = 14$

$8 \times 2 = 16$

$9 \times 2 = 18$

$10 \times 2 = 20$

$11 \times 2 = 22$

$12 \times 2 = 24$

0 2 4 6 8 10 12 14 16 18 20 22 24

Tables on parade

The sergeant major is drilling his troops and they must learn to march in time and chant their tables!

★ Choose a times table to practise, eg the three times table. Choose a sergeant major who will point to an enlarged copy of the chosen times table using a stick. The rest of the class take the role of the troops, standing tall and straight, marching on the spot in time with the beat.

★ Play performance track 13 and chant the table followed by its multiples, eg

> *Zero times three is zero,*
> *One times three is three...*

★ When the children are confident with the chosen table, perform it from memory with backing track 14. The sergeant major can conduct the troops using the stick or beat time on a drum.

EXTENDING THE ACTIVITY

★ In a large space, perform the chosen times table in rows, marching up and down.

★ When the children know several times tables, allow the sergeant major to choose which one the troops will practise. When the children are confident, use the backing track and remove any displays so that the children perform entirely from memory.

★ To test the children's tables knowledge, you or a confident child can take the role of sergeant major to call out a calculation for the children to answer, eg

Sergeant major:	Troops:
Nine times three.	*Twenty-seven.*
Eleven times three.	*Thirty-three.*

★ Use the backing track to keep the pace going. Extend to use other vocabulary and include division calculations, eg 24 shared by 3.

WHAT YOU WILL NEED

★ An enlarged copy of the chosen times table songsheet if needed (opposite or relevant songsheet on CD)

★ A stick

★ A drum for beating time (optional)

Extension activity:

★ Space to march up and down

Teaching focus
• Any times table.

SINGING TIMES TABLES BOOK 1 • HELEN MACGREGOR & STEPHEN CHADWICK © 2013 A&C BLACK PUBLISHERS LTD • www.bloomsbury.com/music

Tables on parade
Example: three times table

Sergeant major and troops:

$0 \times 3 = 0$

$1 \times 3 = 3$

$2 \times 3 = 6$

$3 \times 3 = 9$

$4 \times 3 = 12$

$5 \times 3 = 15$

$6 \times 3 = 18$

$7 \times 3 = 21$

$8 \times 3 = 24$

$9 \times 3 = 27$

$10 \times 3 = 30$

$11 \times 3 = 33$

$12 \times 3 = 36$

0 3 6 9 12 15 18 21 24 27 30 33 36

Robot X

Robot X needs to practise its times tables in order to make calculations. Choose any times table you are learning and chant it using a robotic voice.

★ Choose a times table to practise, eg the four times table. Display an enlarged copy of the chosen times table if needed. Make yourself look like a metal robot with stiff arms, necks and legs. Play performance track 15 and practise making simple robot-like movements in time with the beat:
>   1) jerk right arm up
>   2) jerk right arm down
>   3) jerk left arm up
>   4) jerk left arm down.

★ Play the performance track again, repeating the robot moves together, chanting the times table followed by its multiples in a robotic voice along with the robot on the track.

> *Zero times four is zero,*
> *One times four is four…*

EXTENDING THE ACTIVITY

★ Find a large space where the children can move around like robots to backing track 16, chanting the chosen table.

★ Play this *Robot* game: make a model robot from cardboard boxes and the robot face template (p52 and CD). Paint buttons and dials on the robot and cut out a mouth to post cards through.

Make a set of cards to test the children's tables knowledge, eg 5 x 10 = ?

Choose one child to hold the model and take the role of the robot. A second child chooses a card, reads it to the class, then posts it into the robot's mouth. The class chant 'Tell us the answer, robot'. The robot then calls out the answer in a robotic voice to check with the class that the answer is correct.

WHAT YOU WILL NEED

★ An enlarged copy of the chosen times table songsheet if needed (opposite or relevant songsheet on the CD)

Extension activity:

★ Cardboard boxes and paints

★ Robot face template (p52 and CD)

Teaching focus
• Any times table.

Robot X

Example: four times table

0 x 4 = 0
1 x 4 = 4
2 x 4 = 8
3 x 4 = 12
4 x 4 = 16
5 x 4 = 20
6 x 4 = 24
7 x 4 = 28
8 x 4 = 32
9 x 4 = 36
10 x 4 = 40
11 x 4 = 44
12 x 4 = 48

0   4   8   12   16   20   24   28   32   36   40   44   48

Copycat mice

The cat prowls around the house thinking of all the mouse families he is going to eat. But the mice are too clever to be caught and tease him by copying everything he says!

★ Choose a times table to practise based on the number of mice in each family, eg a mouse family of five to practise the five times table. You take the role of the cat and ask the children to be the mice.

Listen to performance track 17 and join in with the cat's voice as it starts. The mice copy you using their squeaky, high-pitched mice voices!

Cat:	Mice:
Zero times five is zero,	*Zero times five is zero,*
One times five is five...	*One times five is five...*

Join together to chant the multiples.

★ Move like a cat as you chant – make paws and claws with your hands and 'prowl' in time with the beat. The mice may make little paws and groom their whiskers!

EXTENDING THE ACTIVITY

★ Using backing track 18, ask more confident groups of children to take the role of the cat while everyone else echoes as the mice. A confident individual could lead the chant on their own.

★ As a class or in groups of three, practise the two times tables with the backing track using cat and mouse masks that the children have made (p53 and CD) to act out the chant as you say it.

★ Explore tables by asking the children to draw sets of mouse families of different numbers then chant the relevant times table.

WHAT YOU WILL NEED

★ An enlarged copy of the chosen times table songsheet if needed (opposite or relevant songsheet on the CD)

Extension activity:

★ Cat and mouse masks (p53 and CD)

★ Pens and paper for the children to draw mouse families

Teaching focus
• Any times table.

SINGING TIMES TABLES BOOK 1 • HELEN MACGREGOR & STEPHEN CHADWICK © 2013 A&C BLACK PUBLISHERS LTD • www.bloomsbury.com/music

Copycat mice

Example: five times table

Cat:

0 x 5 = 0

1 x 5 = 5

2 x 5 = 10

3 x 5 = 15

4 x 5 = 20

5 x 5 = 25

6 x 5 = 30

7 x 5 = 35

8 x 5 = 40

9 x 5 = 45

10 x 5 = 50

11 x 5 = 55

12 x 5 = 60

Mice:

0 x 5 = 0

1 x 5 = 5

2 x 5 = 10

3 x 5 = 15

4 x 5 = 20

5 x 5 = 25

6 x 5 = 30

7 x 5 = 35

8 x 5 = 40

9 x 5 = 45

10 x 5 = 50

11 x 5 = 55

12 x 5 = 60

Cat and mice:

0 (0)   5 (5)   10 (10)   15 (15)   20 (20)   25 (25)

30 (30)   35 (35)   40 (40)   45 (45)   50 (50)

55 (55)   60 (60)

Ghost hunt

The ghost buster is on a mission to clean a haunted house. She must creep around with her special ghost-proof vacuum cleaner, hoovering up twelve ghosts. Each ghost appears, one by one, from a different hiding place. The ghost buster must calculate the power setting for the vacuum in order to eliminate all twelve.

★ Choose a times table to practise, eg the ten times table. To hoover up one ghost, the ghostbuster needs a vacuum power setting of 10. Two ghosts will need a setting of 20, and so on. Display an enlarged copy of the chosen times table if needed.

★ Play performance track 19 and creep on the spot in time with the beat. Join in with the ghost's voice on the first number of each sum, then continue chanting the rest of the sum:

> *Zero times ten is zero,*
> *One times ten is ten...*

EXTENDING THE ACTIVITY

★ Make a class wall display of the haunted house and make twelve ghosts using the templates (p54 and CD). Decide on a hiding place for each ghost in the haunted house. Number the ghosts from 1 to 12 to show the route around the house. Using a sticky note, add the power setting needed to eliminate each ghost to remind the children of the multiples.

★ Perform the ten times table with backing track 20, using the display as a reminder of the multiples. Remove the multiples and repeat entirely from memory.

★ Perform the chant with other times tables, setting the imaginary machine to the matching power number. Can the children add the correct multiples for the new table to the haunted house display?

★ When they are confident, perform the tables chant without prompts. To test the table, point to a numbered ghost on the display and ask the children to give you the power setting for the chosen multiplication sum.

WHAT YOU WILL NEED

★ An enlarged copy of the chosen times table songsheet if needed (opposite or relevant songsheet on the CD)

Extension activity:

★ Materials for making a wall display of a haunted house

★ Twelve ghosts (p54 and CD)

★ Sticky notes for removable power labels

Teaching focus
• Any times table.

SINGING TIMES TABLES BOOK 1 • HELEN MACGREGOR & STEPHEN CHADWICK © 2013 A&C BLACK PUBLISHERS LTD • www.bloomsbury.com/music

Ghost hunt

Example: ten times table

0 x 10 =   0
1 x 10 = 10
2 x 10 = 20
3 x 10 = 30
4 x 10 = 40
5 x 10 = 50
6 x 10 = 60
7 x 10 = 70
8 x 10 = 80
9 x 10 = 90
10 x 10 = 100
11 x 10 = 110
12 x 10 = 120

0 10 20 30 40 50 60 70 80 90
100 110 120

Zero to eleven

PERFORMANCE 21 **BACKING** 22 55

A monkey comes to visit and gets up to all kinds of tricks involving numbers from zero to eleven. First he sorts them in evens, and then in odds.

★ Display a number line, 0–11, and the songsheet (opposite and CD) where everyone can see them. Play performance track 21, demonstrating the actions suggested by the words as you all listen.

★ Play the performance track again, inviting the children to join in with the actions. Can the children describe the number patterns? (Three numbers per verse, increasing in twos. The first four verses begin with three even numbers. The other four verses begin with three odd numbers.)

★ Circle the even numbers on the number line and put a triangle around the odd numbers, or colour them in using two different colours.

★ Play the performance track, all joining in with the numbers including the sequence of even numbers 0–10 and odd numbers 1–11.

★ Finally, learn all the words one verse at a time, then perform the song and actions with backing track 22.

EXTENDING THE ACTIVITY

★ Practise number recognition and recall of the counting patterns by playing this *Monkey* game: hold up cards showing the three numbers from each verse, eg 6 8 10 (p55 and CD). Can the children identify the numbers and say the rhyming words of the matching verse? (*Monkey's back again.*)

★ When the children are confident and know the song well, mix up the verses by holding up the groups of three numbers from each verse in a different order. Perform the new version of the song to the backing track.

WHAT YOU WILL NEED

★ An enlarged copy of the songsheet (opposite and CD)

★ Materials to create a number line

★ Number group cards (p55 and CD)

Teaching focus
• Counting in twos.
• Even numbers/odd numbers from 0–11.

SINGING TIMES TABLES BOOK 1 • HELEN MACGREGOR & STEPHEN CHADWICK © 2013 A&C BLACK PUBLISHERS LTD • www.bloomsbury.com/mus

Zero to eleven

Zero two four,
Who's that at my door?
I hear a knock,
I'll turn the lock,
0 2 4.

Two four six,
Monkey's playing tricks,
He jumped on me,
Then climbed a tree,
2 4 6.

Four six eight,
Monkey's on the gate,
He bends his knees,
Then scratches fleas,
4 6 8.

Six eight ten,
Monkey's back again,
He pinched my food ~
How very rude!
6 8 10.

0 2 4 6 8 10

One three five,
Monkey takes a dive,
He likes to swim,
It keeps him slim!
1 3 5.

Three five seven,
Monkey's down in Devon,
He's gone away on holiday,
3 5 7.

Five seven nine,
Monkey's feeling fine,
He's home with me,
In time for tea,
5 7 9.

Seven nine eleven,
Monkey's back in Devon,
He's taking me to see the sea!
7 9 11.

1 3 5 7 9 11

Two by two

PERFORMANCE 23 BACKING 24

Noah counts pairs of animals into the ark to save them from the flood. When they reach dry land he lets them go, two at a time, until the ark is empty.

★ Remind the children of the story of Noah's ark.

★ Display an enlarged copy of the songsheet (opposite and CD).

★ Listen to performance track 23 and ask the children if they can remember the five pairs of animals in the chant.

★ Use the small world animals to illustrate the sequence of animals, ensuring that the children understand that multiplying is the same as a sequence of additions, eg 4 x 2 is the same as 2 + 2 + 2 + 2.

★ Learn the verses, gradually joining in with the performance track until the children are confident enough to chant with backing track 24.

★ Give everyone a role in the story, including Noah and his family, and mime the building of the ark. Use toy animals or animal masks to enact the process of the animals being counted into and out of the ark, while everyone chants.

WHAT YOU WILL NEED

★ An enlarged copy of the songsheet (opposite and CD)

★ Pairs of small world toy animals

★ Materials to make your own animal masks

EXTENDING THE ACTIVITY

★ Ask small groups of children to create new sequences of animal pairs using five new pairs of toy animals.

★ Extend the number sequence by introducing five further pairs of toy animals and continue counting in twos up to 20 and back to 0 as the animals leave the ark.

Teaching focus
• Counting in twos from 2–10.
• Understanding that the two times table is the same as a sequence consisting of the addition of twos.

Two by two

Noah built an ark, a big wooden boat,
He collected many creatures and hoped it'd float.
Whether furry or hairy, or fat or thin,
He lined them up in twos and marched them in.

A pair of doves first, in they flew, and that made two.
Two tiny ants crawled under the door, and that made four.
Next, two chimpanzees playing tricks, and that made six.
Elephant stomped in beside her mate, and that made eight.
The foxes fleeing from their deep, flooded den, and that made ten.
Two by two, by two by two,
Filling up the ark ~ what a hullabaloo!

Then the sky grew dark and the raindrops fell,
But Noah kept the creatures safe and well.
When the storm was over, they could see blue sky,
And they all left the ark 'cos the land was dry.
Foxes ~ 10, elephants ~ 8, chimpanzees ~ 6, ants ~ 4, doves ~ 2
10 8 6 4 2
Two by two, by two by two,
No one left ~ no more hullabaloo!

Jangle triangle

Jangle your triangles as you sing and count the increasing numbers of sides as more triangles join the band.

★ Ask the children to identify the number of sides of a triangle. Display the songsheet (opposite and CD) and say the lyrics of the first verse together.

★ Give out the triangles (p56 and CD) to twelve children and ask them to stand in a line. The first child holds up their triangle and everyone calls out the number of sides. Continue to the end of the line adding triangles one by one and working out the total number of sides as you go.

★ Next, perform the whole sequence with performance track 25, calling out the answer after each triangle 'ting' and chanting the multiples at the end.

Singer:	Children:
One triangle ~	*Three,*
Two triangles ~	*Six...*

★ Learn the whole song and when the children are confident, sing with backing track 26.

WHAT YOU WILL NEED

★ An enlarged copy of the songsheet (opposite and CD)

★ Twelve triangles (instruments or shapes) or twelve card cut-outs of triangles (p56 and CD)

EXTENDING THE ACTIVITY

★ With or without the backing track, mix up the order in which you call out the number of triangles to test the children's knowledge of the three times table, eg

You:	Children:
Five triangles ~	*Fifteen,*
Ten triangles ~	*Thirty...*

★ As the children line up to go out to play, use the song to practise their three times tables, tailoring it for individual abilities. As they line up, sing one song line to each child – if they get the correct answer, they go out to play; if not, the next in line gets a chance to answer and go out. The first child tries again, and the game continues until everyone has gone out to play.

Teaching focus
• Three times table – understanding and sequence.
• Multiples of three.

Jangle triangle

Jingle jungle jangle
Three sides ~ a triangle!
Jingle jungle jangle
Three sides ~ a triangle!

One triangle ~   3
Two triangles ~   6
Three triangles ~   9
Multiply by three!
Hey, hey, hey!

Four triangles ~   12
Five triangles ~   15
Six triangles ~   18
Multiply by three!
Hey, hey, hey!

Seven triangles ~   21
Eight triangles ~   24
Nine triangles ~   27
Multiply by three!
Hey, hey, hey!

Ten triangles ~   30
Eleven triangles ~   33
Twelve triangles ~   36
Multiply by three!
Hey, hey, hey!

3	6	9
12	15	18
21	24	27
30	33	36

Yeah! And now we're done!

Monkey business

Two hungry monkeys are busy picking bananas for their tea. They can hold a bunch of five bananas in each hand. As they collect the bananas, more pairs of monkeys join the troop. Help them count in multiples of fives up to one hundred.

★ Show the children the banana cards (p56 and CD), noting that each bunch contains five bananas.

★ Display the songsheet (opposite and CD) and listen to performance track 27, inviting the children to join in with the monkey chant (*Hoo ha hoo ha, hee hee hee*) and the number sequence.

★ Learn the verses one at a time, discussing the numbers of monkeys and bananas in each. Notice how the number sequence grows longer in each verse and practise counting each one.

★ When confident, sing the whole song with backing track 28.

★ Give two children two banana cards each. Invite the children with the banana cards to play the part of the monkeys and act out the first verse of the song. During the number sequence, each of the children holds up both cards, one in their left and one in their right hand, as the rest of the class count in fives to find out the total. Repeat with four children, and so on.

EXTENDING THE ACTIVITY

★ Explore the mathematics in the song: what is the pattern of the number of monkeys in each verse; how many bananas does each monkey have?

★ Sing the song as a mental arithmetic challenge. Sing the first line of one verse to the children, eg *Eight monkeys swinging in a tree*. Let the children sing the counting section.

Ask the children what strategies they have used to work out the answer, eg one monkey has ten bananas, so eight monkeys have eighty bananas (8 x 10 = 80).

★ Change the number of bananas in a bunch to practise other times tables, eg two monkeys with three bananas in each hand: 3 6 9 12.

WHAT YOU WILL NEED

★ An enlarged copy of the songsheet (opposite and CD)

★ Banana cards (p56 and CD) or design your own cards with five bananas on each

Teaching focus
• Counting in fives to one hundred.
• Multiplication facts.

Monkey business

Two monkeys swinging in a tree,
Finding bananas for their tea.
Pick bananas, down they land,
Five bananas in each hand:
5 10 15 20,
Hoo ha hoo ha, hee hee hee.
Twenty bananas for their tea,
Hoo ha hoo ha, hee hee hee.

Four monkeys swinging in a tree...
5 10 15 20 25 30 35 40,
Hoo ha hoo ha, hee hee hee.
Forty bananas for their tea,
Hoo ha hoo ha, hee hee hee.

Six monkeys swinging in a tree...
5 10 15 20 25 30 35 40
45 50 55 60,
Hoo ha hoo ha, hee hee hee.
Sixty bananas for their tea,
Hoo ha hoo ha, hee hee hee.

Eight monkeys swinging in a tree...
5 10 15 20 25 30 35 40
45 50 55 60 65 70 75 80,
Hoo ha hoo ha, hee hee hee.
Eighty bananas for their tea,
Hoo ha hoo ha, hee hee hee.

Ten monkeys swinging in a tree...
5 10 15 20 25 30 35 40
45 50 55 60 65 70 75 80
85 90 95 100,
Hoo ha hoo ha, hee hee hee.
One hundred bananas for their tea,
Hoo ha hoo ha, hee hee hee.

Pond life

Down at the pond you can hear number patterns in the sounds of the creatures that live there. Listen as a frog croaks, a bee buzzes, a duck quacks and a fish blows bubbles, then make the sounds with your voices.

★ Show the children an enlarged copy of the number grid (p57 and CD). Play performance track 29 and point to each number in turn as you count from one to fifty together, keeping in time with the beat.

★ Listen again, counting silently this time. What do the children notice about the music? (There are animal sounds on some numbers.)

★ Play the performance track again. Which animal sound can they hear on the multiples of two? (The frog.) Add cut-out frogs (p57 and CD) to the multiples of two on the display to match the sound pattern. All join in with the frog sounds on the performance track as you follow the numbers and frogs on the grid.

★ Play backing track 30 to chant the even number pattern. Can the children describe the pattern of numbers which have no frog cut-outs on them? (They also go up in twos – 1 3 5 7 etc, they are odd numbers.)

★ Listen out, one by one, for the sound patterns for the bee (3s), duck (4s) and fish (5s). Use the number grid and cut-out animals to highlight each number pattern. Discuss and explore the patterns by performing each animal's sound with the vocal track and the number pattern with the backing track.

EXTENDING THE ACTIVITIES

★ Play this *Animal patterns* game: divide the class into two animal groups, eg frogs and bees. Combine the two vocal sound patterns (two times and three times table) using either the performance or backing track. Discuss the way the patterns combine.

★ Play the *Animal patterns* game with instruments, eg frog – scrapers, fish – egg shaker, bee – finger cymbals, duck – claves.

★ Compose your own times tables grid music. Choose another theme eg transport, and perform with vocal sounds or instruments.

★ Continue exploring the number patterns on a 100-square grid.

WHAT YOU WILL NEED

★ An enlarged copy of the songsheet (p57 and CD)

★ Animal templates (p57 and CD)

Extension activity:

★ At least four different percussion instruments, eg scrapers, egg shakers, finger cymbals, claves

Teaching focus
• Any times table.
• Recognition of numbers.
• Investigating patterns.

Pond life

0	1	2	3	4	5	6	7	8	9	10
11	12	13	14	15	16	17	18	19		20
21	22	23	24	25	26	27	28	29		30
31	32	33	34	35	36	37	38	39		40
41	42	43	44	45	46	47	48	49		50

Hoedown on the tables

PERFORMANCE
31

BACKING
32

58

Have fun at the local barn dance performing a hoedown which helps practise the two times table.

★ Show the children the songsheet (opposite and CD) and the hoedown dance steps display (p58 and CD) or simplify/adapt the moves as appropriate to your class.

★ Play performance track 31, demonstrating the hoedown dance steps so that the children can copy and join in. Notice how the test questions are set in the chant section, ending with the hat twirling.

★ Perform the whole song with dance moves using the times tables examples given on the performance track. When the children are confident with the song, use backing track 32 to set your own questions based on the two times table so that the class can call out the answers in time with the music.

EXTENDING THE ACTIVITY

★ Reverse the tables questions so that the children understand that, eg $2 \times 4 = 8$ is the same as $4 \times 2 = 8$.

★ Perform the hoedown in an assembly to celebrate the children's learning of the two times table!

★ Working in small groups, the children can invent their own hoedown dance moves to perform with the song. Use these to practise recall of other tables.

Each individual group can select a times table to challenge the rest of the class. They decide on the questions they will ask in the testing sections of the song, and the class responds with the answers.

WHAT YOU WILL NEED

★ An enlarged copy of the songsheet (opposite and CD)

★ Hoedown dance moves display (p58 and CD)

Teaching focus
• Testing knowledge and recall of any times table.

Hoedown on the tables
Example: two times table

Hands on hips.
Ready!
How-de-do!

Leader:	Group:
2 x 2?	4
2 x 6?	12
2 x 10?	20

Bend those knees.
Steady!
Yes, we do!

Yee-ha! Yee-ha! You bet we do!

Times tables hoedown.
How-de-do! *(repeat actions)*
We know our two times tables.
Yes, we do!
Times tables hoedown.
How-de-do!
Yee-ha! Yee-ha!
You bet we do!

Step to the music.
How-de-do!

Yee-ha! Yee-ha!
You bet we do!

Leader:	Group:
2 x 5?	10
2 x 9?	18
2 x 3?	6

Times tables hoedown.
How-de-do! *(repeat actions)*
We know our two times tables.
Yes, we do!
Times tables hoedown.
How-de-do!
Yee-ha! Yee-ha! You bet we do!

Yee-ha! Yee-ha! You bet we do!

Times tables hoedown…

(repeat actions)

SINGING TIMES TABLES BOOK 1 • HELEN MACGREGOR & STEPHEN CHADWICK © 2013 A&C BLACK PUBLISHERS LTD • www.bloomsbury.com/music

Brainwaves

This song gives the opportunity to test the children's mental recall of any times tables they have learnt.

★ Display the songsheet (opposite and CD) where everyone can see it. Listen to performance track 33 to learn the melody and to hear how the testing section works.

★ Select a times table to practise. Play backing track 34 as you sing the verses together. Call out four multiplication sums for the class to answer in each testing section. If you prefer, they can write down their answers individually, then hold them up and call out their answers as you all sing the song a second time.

EXTENDING THE ACTIVITY

★ Play *Tables bingo*. Give the children blank bingo cards (p59 and CD).

Select a times table to practise, eg the five times table. Ask the children to think of six answers to multiplication sums from the chosen times table and write them on their grid:

❋ BINGO ❋	
5	25
10	30
20	50

Sing the song together. This time, as you call out the sums, the children cross off any correct answers from those they have chosen to put on their bingo cards. When all the numbers have been crossed off on a card, the player shouts 'bingo!' If there is no winner at the end, repeat the song.

★ As the children learn more tables, include a mixture of them in the song or in the *Tables bingo* game.

WHAT YOU WILL NEED

★ An enlarged copy of the songsheet (opposite and CD)

★ Paper and pens for writing down the answers to multiplication sums (optional)

Extension activity:

★ Blank bingo cards for each child (p59 and CD) and pens

Teaching focus
• Testing knowledge and recall of any times table.

Brainwaves
Example: five times table

Signals flowing through my brain, faster than a high-speed train;
Never late, never slow! Testing tables, off we go!

Leader:	Group:
5 x 0?	0
5 x 8?	40
5 x 4?	20
5 x 10?	50

Signals flowing through my brain, faster than a high-speed train;
Speeding out along the tracks, now I know my number facts.
Signals flowing through my brain, faster than a high-speed train;
Never late, never slow! Testing tables, off we go!

Leader:	Group:
5 x 12?	60
5 x 3?	15
5 x 1?	5
5 x 2?	10

Signals flowing through my brain, faster than a high-speed train;
Speeding out along the tracks, now I know my number facts.

Sound effects tables

This song has sound effects designed to prompt recall of tricky times tables.

★ Display the sound effects chart (opposite, p60 and CD) and explain that each sound effect will be followed by a multiplication sum. Listen to the example on performance track 35.

★ The children join in making the sound effects and chanting the sums, eg *Woof woof woof woof woof, Woof woof woof woof woof. Twelve times three is thirty-six.*

★ Perform the sound effects and chants several times with backing track 36. Talk about the sums and the sound effects, and ask the children to imagine ways to relate the sound effects to the sums (eg 22 aircraft flying by: 11 x 2 = 22, 48 lions roaring: 12 x 4 = 48). Add actions for each to make the sums more multi-sensory and therefore easier to memorise.

EXTENDING THE ACTIVITY

★ Play version 1 or version 2 of this *Sound effects* game to practise and memorise the sums.

★ Version 1: Display an enlarged version of the sound effects chart (p60 and CD). Choose a confident child to make one of the sound effects. The class respond by chanting the corresponding sum, eg

| Child laughs: | *Haha haha* |
| Class respond: | *9 x 4 = 36* |

Version 2: Display a blank sound effects chart (p61 and CD). Ask the children to think of nine sums they find difficult to remember and write them in the right-hand column. Ask the children to think up sound effects or actions to go before each sum (eg clapping, cat meow, buzzer sound, patting knees, waving arms etc) and add them to the left-hand column next to the corresponding sum.

Perform the sequence of sound effects and multiplication sums with the backing track. Repeat using different sound effects and sums.

WHAT YOU WILL NEED

★ An enlarged version of the sound effects chart (opposite, p60 and CD)

Extension activity:

★ A blank version of the sound effects chart (p61 and CD)

Teaching focus
• Memorising and recalling individual table facts.

Sound effects tables

Sound effect	Multiplication sum
bark	12 x 3 = 36
boing boing	8 x 2 = 16
police	2 x 3 = 6
roar	12 x 4 = 48
cluck cluck	3 x 5 = 15
honk	11 x 10 = 110
flush	5 x 5 = 25
zoom	11 x 2 = 22
haa haa	9 x 4 = 36

Echoes

In this activity, the times tables are chanted backwards instead of forwards, eg starting with 12 x 2, then 11 x 2 and finishing with 0 x 2.

★ Divide the class into three groups: a lead group and two echo groups. Display the songsheet (opposite and CD) where everyone can follow as they chant with performance track 37.

★ The lead group chants the times table. The first echo group repeats the answer more quietly, followed by the second echo group, more quietly still. Repeat, swapping groups so that each has an opportunity to take the lead.

★ To simplify, you may prefer to divide the class into two groups, each chanting the whole sum, with alternative performance track 38:

Group 1:
12 x 2 = 24
11 x 2 = 22

Group 2:
12 x 2 = 24
11 x 2 = 22

★ When the children know the times table backwards, hide the answers from view so that the children have to recall them from memory, eg 12 x 2 = ?, 11 x 2 = ? etc

EXTENDING THE ACTIVITY

★ Choose an individual child to be the leader, with the rest of the class divided into two echo groups. This time, the leader uses different vocal qualities, eg squeaky mouse, low giant, spooky ghost, monotonal robot. The echo groups copy the vocal quality.

★ Select another times table to practise backwards, eg the three times table. Play backing track 39 and show the children a copy of the table with the answers to refer to as they chant in three groups.

★ Test the children's knowledge by giving them each a worksheet (p62 and CD) with the answers removed. This time, as they listen to the backing track, the children chant the sums shown on the worksheet, then write down the answer to each.

Perform the chant again as the children read out the answers they have written.

★ To challenge the children further, combine two or more tables in mixed up order, eg 12 x 5 = ?, 10 x 10 = ? etc

WHAT YOU WILL NEED

Extension activity:

★ An enlarged copy of your chosen backwards times table complete with answers

★ Copies of the backwards number chart worksheet to give to the children (p62 and CD)

la la l

Teaching focus
• Testing knowledge of tables facts.

Echoes

Example: two times table

	Echo 1:	Echo 2:
12 x 2 = 24	24	24
11 x 2 = 22	22	22
10 x 2 = 20	20	20
9 x 2 = 18	18	18
8 x 2 = 16	16	16
7 x 2 = 14	14	14
6 x 2 = 12	12	12
5 x 2 = 10	10	10
4 x 2 = 8	8	8
3 x 2 = 6	6	6
2 x 2 = 4	4	4
1 x 2 = 2	2	2
0 x 2 = 0	0	0

In reverse

PERFORMANCE 40   BACKING 41   63

In this game the children practise their tables in reverse and learn that the numbers 'balance' on both sides of the equals sign. They are given an answer number and use their tables knowledge to identify corresponding multiplication sums, eg 12 = 1 x 12, or 12 x 1, or 2 x 6, etc.

★ To introduce the game, write all eight answers from the examples opposite on the board, each followed by an equals sign. Next, write the multiplication sums in a mixed-up list on the right-hand side.

★ Play performance track 40 and call out each answer as demonstrated in the recording.

★ Using backing track 41, ask the children to join in singing the word '*equals*' as they find and call out the correct multiplication sum after the cue 'plink plink plink'. Join the answers to the matching sums. To make the game easier, the class need not join in singing '*equals*' so they have more time to find the correct sum.

★ Next, write the correct answers next to the correct multiplication sums. Ask the children if they can find any other multiplication sums to match the answers, eg 10 = 2 x 5, or 1 x 10, or 10 x 1. Write down their suggestions to the right of the original sums. Play the backing track, asking individual children to call out a correct multiplication sum from those on the board to match the answer number on the track, tailoring the questions to match their abilities.

EXTENDING THE ACTIVITY

★ Play the *Number grid* game: select a times table, eg the five times table. Give the children individual number grid worksheets (p63 and CD).

Ask the class to select eight answer numbers and write them on the board, eg 20, 40, 15, 55, 10, 25, 60, 35.

Play the backing track, calling out the answer numbers one by one. The children find one place on their grid to write in the answer number, eg 20 could be placed on 4 x 5, or 5 x 4, or 10 x 2, or 2 x 10.

At the end of the song, play the backing track again, inviting individual children to call out the multiplication sum they have recorded. Collect other possible multiplication sums in the same way, completing a composite grid that the class can see.

WHAT YOU WILL NEED

Extension activity:

★ A blank number grid worksheet for each child (p63 and CD)

Teaching focus
• Testing knowledge and recall of any times table.
• Products and factors.

In reverse

Example:

10 =	1 x 4
4 =	3 x 5
8 =	10 x 5
9 =	11 x 2
15 =	4 x 2
50 =	3 x 3
22 =	3 x 4
12 =	5 x 2

Milk bottle deliveries

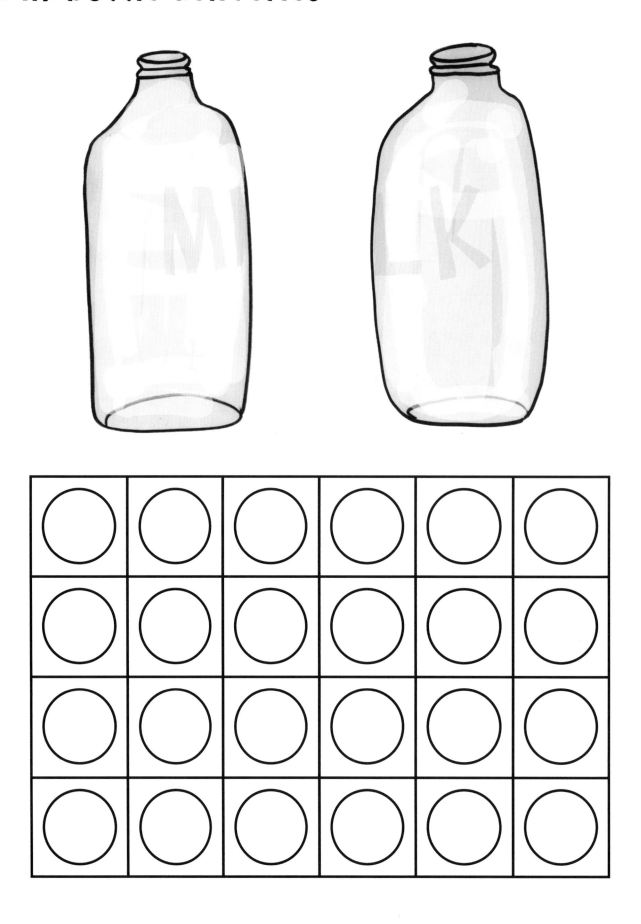

Milk bottle deliveries

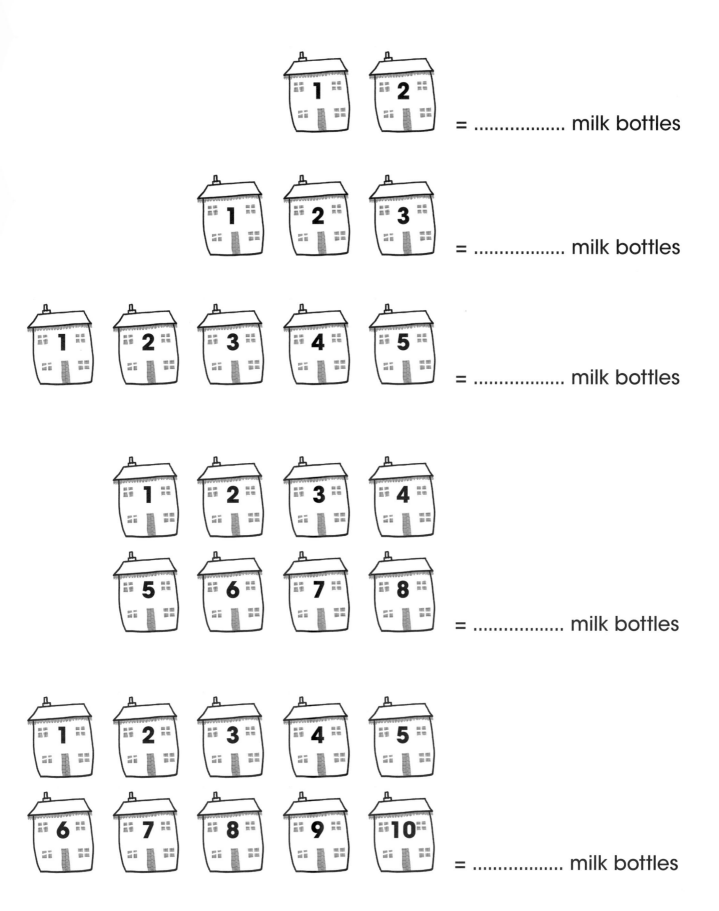

= .... milk bottles

= .... milk bottles

= .... milk bottles

= .... milk bottles

= .... milk bottles

Three is a magic number

January	
February	
March	
April	
May	
June	
July	
August	
September	
October	
November	
December	

Procession of four-legged beasts

Five finger-snakes

SINGING TIMES TABLES BOOK 1 • HELEN MACGREGOR & STEPHEN CHADWICK © 2013 A&C BLACK PUBLISHERS LTD • www.bloomsbury.com/musi

Finger-fish

The giant's table

Robot X

SINGING TIMES TABLES BOOK 1 • HELEN MACGREGOR & STEPHEN CHADWICK © 2013 A&C BLACK PUBLISHERS LTD • www.bloomsbury.com/mus

Copycat mice

Ghost hunt

SINGING TIMES TABLES BOOK 1 • HELEN MACGREGOR & STEPHEN CHADWICK © 2013 A&C BLACK PUBLISHERS LTD • www.bloomsbury.com/musi

Zero to eleven

0 2 4	2 4 6
4 6 8	6 8 10
1 3 5	3 5 7
5 7 9	7 9 11

Jangle triangle

Monkey business

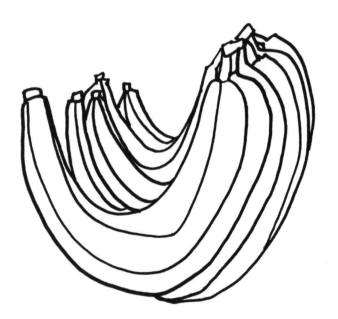 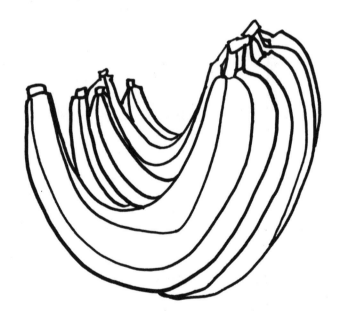

SINGING TIMES TABLES BOOK 1 • HELEN MACGREGOR & STEPHEN CHADWICK © 2013 A&C BLACK PUBLISHERS LTD • www.bloomsbury.com/music

Pond life

0	1	2	3	4	5	6	7	8	9	10
	11	12	13	14	15	16	17	18	19	20
	21	22	23	24	25	26	27	28	29	30
	31	32	33	34	35	36	37	38	39	40
	41	42	43	44	45	46	47	48	49	50

Hoedown on the tables

1. Hands on hips:

2. Bend knees:

3. Step forward, right-left; step back, right-left:

4. Twirl imaginary cowboy hat in the air:

SINGING TIMES TABLES BOOK 1 • HELEN MACGREGOR & STEPHEN CHADWICK © 2013 A&C BLACK PUBLISHERS LTD • www.bloomsbury.com/music

Brainwaves

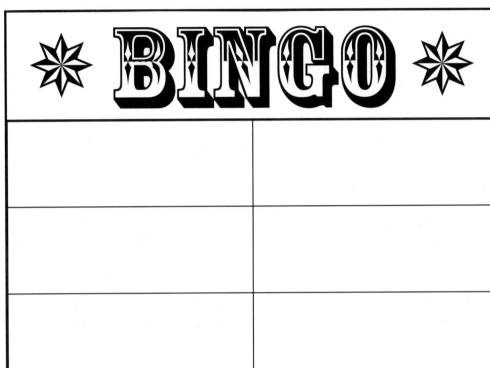

Sound effects tables

Sound effect	Multiplication sum
bark	12 x 3 = 36
boing boing	8 x 2 = 16
police	2 x 3 = 6
roar	12 x 4 = 48
cluck cluck	3 x 5 = 15
honk	11 x 10 = 110
flush	5 x 5 = 25
zoom	11 x 2 = 22
haa haa	9 x 4 = 36

SINGING TIMES TABLES BOOK 1 • HELEN MACGREGOR & STEPHEN CHADWICK © 2013 A&C BLACK PUBLISHERS LTD • www.bloomsbury.com/music

Sound effects tables

Sound effect	Multiplication sum

Echoes

12 x ☐ = ☐   4 x ☐ = ☐

11 x ☐ = ☐   3 x ☐ = ☐

10 x ☐ = ☐   2 x ☐ = ☐

9 x ☐ = ☐   1 x ☐ = ☐

8 x ☐ = ☐   0 x ☐ = ☐

7 x ☐ = ☐

6 x ☐ = ☐

5 x ☐ = ☐

la la la

In reverse

1	2	3	4	5	6	7	8	9	10	11	12
2											
3											
4											
5											
6											
7											
8											
9											
10											
11											
12											

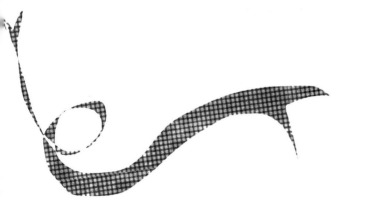 

Song index and CD track list

First published 2013 by A&C Black Publishers Ltd
Bloomsbury Publishing Plc, 49–51 Bedford Square, London, WC1B 3DP
© 2013 A&C Black Publishers Ltd
ISBN 10: 1-408194751
ISBN 13: 978-1-4081-9475-1

Text copyright © 2013 Helen MacGregor, Stephen Chadwick
Songs copyright © 2013 Helen MacGregor, Stephen Chadwick
Edited by Sheena Roberts and Stephanie Matthews
Cover illustration © 2013 Julia Patton
Inside illustrations © 2013 Julia Patton
Vocals performed by Sian Jones and Nigel Pilkington
Backing tracks by Stephen Chadwick
Sound engineering by Stephen Chadwick
CD post-production by Ian Shepherd, Mastering Media

Printed and bound by CPI Group (UK) Ltd, Croydon, CRO 4YY

Acknowledgements
Thanks to Anna, Sheena and Chris Hussey.